You won't believe this but...

John Townsend

Published in association with
The Basic Skills Agency

Hodder Murray

A MEMBER OF THE HODDER HEADLINE GROUP

Photo acknowledgements
p.6 Goldfish bowl © John Angerson/Alamy; p.8 Potato cod © Stephen Frink Collection/
Alamy; p.11 Bengal tiger © Tom Brakefield/Corbis; p.17 Parachutist © Kevin R.
Morris/Corbis; p.20 Sea snake © Aqua Image/Alamy.

Every effort has been made to trace copyright holders of material reproduced in this book.
Any rights not acknowledged will be acknowledged in subsequent printings if notice is
given to the publisher.

Hodder Headline's policy is to use papers that are natural, renewable and recyclable
products and made from wood grown in sustainable forests. The logging and
manufacturing processes are expected to conform to the environmental regulations of the
country of origin.

Orders: please contact Bookpoint Ltd, 130 Milton Park, Abingdon, Oxon OX14 4SB.
Telephone: (44) 01235 827720. Fax: (44) 01235 400454. Lines are open from 9.00am to
5.00pm, Monday to Saturday, with a 24-hour message answering service.
Visit our website at www.hoddereducation.co.uk

© John Townsend 2003, 2006
First published in the Livewire series in 2003 and first published in the Hodder Reading
Project series in 2006 by Hodder Murray, an imprint of Hodder Education, a member of
the Hodder Headline Group, 338 Euston Road, London NW1 3BH.

Impression number   10 9 8 7 6 5 4
Year   2011 2010 2009 2008 2007

Cover photo: Goldfish bowl © Gary Sheppard/Photolibrary.com.
Typeset by SX Composing DTP, Rayleigh, Essex.
Printed in Great Britain by CPI Bath.

A catalogue record for this title is available from the British Library

ISBN-10: 0 340 91574 9
ISBN-13: 978 0340 915 745

Contents

Page

1 A Funny Old World   1

2 Out of the Blue   3

3 Fishy Tales   5

4 Animal Antics   9

5 That was Close   13

6 Nurse . . . Help!   19

7 What a Way to Go   22

8 Almost the End   25

1
A Funny Old World

Odd things happen each day –
things you may not believe.
Newspapers tell stories all the time
that just can't be true.
Or can they?

They say truth is stranger than fiction.
Stories happen every day
that we couldn't make up
– never in our wildest dreams.
There are some stories in the news
you may find hard to believe.

Animals can get up to odd things
but people can be very weird.
They can also be stupid or just unlucky.
You might laugh.
You might think it's all made up.
Or you might want to tell someone.

Most people like to pass on an odd story.
There are plenty to choose from here.
You might begin with:
'You won't believe this but ...'

They might say,
'It's a funny old world out there.'
You'll soon see why.

2
Out of the Blue

Funny things fall from the sky,
things you wouldn't expect.
At a boat race in Mexico in 1968
a strange thing happened.
The sky grew dark.
It began to rain.
People watching from the shore got wet
but the rain turned white.
It turned into live maggots.
Hundreds of fat wriggly maggots
fell from the sky!

In 1979, a lot of frogs fell
from the sky in Bedford.
It seems they were sucked up from a pond
by a strong wind.
The frogs flew up into the clouds,
then they began to rain
and hop into the streets!

In 1984,
it rained in East Ham in London.
This time it was fish.
Perhaps a mini-tornado over the sea
scooped them up.
Then down they came,
lots of them,
just by the fish and chip shop!

One story tells of geese falling
into the streets in 1932.
Lightning hit a flock of geese flying
over Elgin in Canada.
It killed and cooked them in seconds.
The story goes that 52 sizzling birds
dropped from the sky.
People ran to pick up a quick ready meal.
They thought Christmas had come early!

3
Fishy Tales

Did you hear the one about the goldfish
that fell from the sky?
It's true!
It happened in 1999
just before Christmas.
A family sat round the fire one evening
in a cosy home in Northampton.
Suddenly there was a hiss.
They looked up.
A goldfish hit the coal
and dropped on the carpet.
It had come down the chimney!

They stared at the fish.
It gave a flip of its tail.
It was alive!

They got a bowl of water.
It began to swim!
Apart from a few burns it was fine.
Where did it come from?
The R.S.P.C.A. had a few ideas.

Maybe a heron picked up the fish from a pond.
Then maybe the bird sat on the chimney
to eat its meal.
The fish fell from its beak,
and there it was on the carpet.
The fish lived happily ever after!

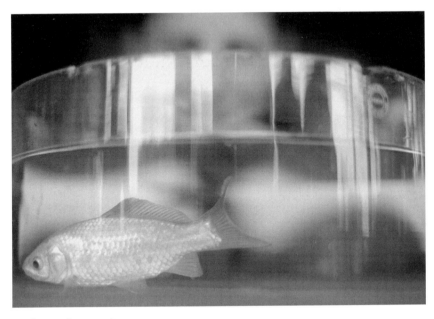

Safe and sound!

A kiss from a pike

Have you gone fishing for a bite?
One man got more than a bite.
He was fishing near Moscow when
he hooked a large pike on his line.
When he got it out of the water,
he held it up for his friends to see.
'Look at this beauty!' he said,
and he gave it a kiss on the mouth.

Pike have lots of teeth,
so it bit him on the nose,
and it didn't let go.
He couldn't get it off.
The man's friends came with a knife.
They cut the pike's head off.
But its mouth stayed shut.
He had to go to hospital
to have the head taken off.
That's quite a kiss!

Cod eats man's head

In 2000 some fishermen had a shock.
It happened in Australia.
They caught a large cod.
They cut it open and a man's head rolled out.
The police had to take it away.

There was a big fuss.
Cod don't eat people!
It may have been the head of a man
who had fallen into the sea
and the cod just sucked it up from the seabed.
Even so, it was a weird fishy tale.

A cod – a bit of a head case!

4
Animal Antics

Man's best friend?
In 1999,
a man drove into the Black Forest in Germany
to go hunting.
In his car he had a loaded gun
and his pet dog.
The 51-year-old man got out of his car
to take a look around.
His dog ran up and down the back seat,
just where the gun was.
The barrel poked out of the window.
The dog's paw hit the trigger.
The shot rang through the woods.
The bullet hit the man and killed him.
The police found him in the mud by his car.
The dog was sitting in the back of the car
still wagging its tail!

The missing hamster

The Cummins family in Alberta
lost a pet hamster.
They couldn't find it anywhere.
When they moved house they knew
they'd never see it again.

But they did.
It returned after they'd moved a second time!

And where was the hamster?
Inside the sofa.
It had dug right into the stuffing
and made a nest.
It lived off scraps that fell down the cracks.
It drank water
from the cat's bowl at night.
It took two years and four months
before he popped out to say 'Hello!'

A bad idea

It was New Year's Day at Calcutta Zoo.
Two men looked at the tiger
asleep in his pen.

'Such a nice cat,' they thought.
They'd been drinking.

'Let's give him a gift,' they said,
and they made a rope out of flowers.

The men swam across the moat.
They climbed up the bank.
'Happy New Year,' they said.
'Wear this round your neck, pussy-cat.'
The tiger woke up.
It wasn't happy ...

Never mess with a tiger!

It knocked them both flat.
With a bite, one was dead
and the other was in a bad way.
Now the tiger could have
a quiet New Year.
It's never wise to wake a tiger!

Stretching the rules

People living on a caravan site
in Hertford were upset.
The council gave them a new rule.
No dogs or cats.
No more than one bird each.
A budgie would be fine.
One man was mad with the council,
and he got his own back.
The next day he brought home
a two-metre tall ostrich.

5
That was Close

Hard to swallow
A three-year-old girl once ate a pound coin.
It got stuck in her throat
and she began to choke.
Her parents couldn't get it out.
She couldn't breathe
so they threw her in the car
and sped off to A & E.

The girl was in a bad way.
It was a race against time.
The car shot up the hill
but couldn't take the bend.
There was a screech and a bang.
A van hit the car.
This was the last thing they needed.

Then the girl sat up on the back seat
and smiled.
The crash had cleared her windpipe.
She could breathe!
A passing car took her to Leeds Hospital
where they took out the coin.
She was fine, but the car wasn't.
It was a write-off.

Blowing a fuse
Drum Major Steven Harding
went a bit 'over the top' in the USA.
He was leading the band in great style.
He threw his baton high into the air
as the crowd cheered,
but he threw it too high.
It hit some power lines and 4,000 volts went wild.
So did the crowd.
They got a free firework show!
A ten-block area was blacked out,
a radio station was blown off the air,
and sparks set off a grass fire.

And his baton?
It melted!

A human pie

Mike worked in a food factory
in County Durham.
In 1994, he fell into a huge food mincer
which cut up the meat for all the pies.

Steel blades spun round at great speed.
One almost cut off his hand.
Another just missed his head.
He was about to be mashed into pie mix
when the alarm went off.
The motor stopped.
It took over an hour
to get Mike out of the huge mixer.
He went to hospital
where they stitched his hand back.
He was lucky not to end up in a real stew!

Chef in a stew

Kim Won-Sun was a chef in the USA.
He was almost cooked alive
when his car crashed in 1989.
He was driving at 60 mph when a tyre burst.
His car spun across the road,
through a fence, and over a bridge.

The car fell 10 metres, onto its roof.
It landed on the electric railway line.
Kim hung from his seat belt as 750 volts
fizzed through the car.

The roof began to melt.
He felt as if he was on a spit-roast.
Then the train came.
It was the express, going at full speed.
It rammed the car and flung it half a mile
down the track.
The car was smashed to bits.
The door fell off and Kim rolled out.
He got to his feet,
and trod on the electric rail.
Luckily, he didn't fry to death.
Just a few seconds before,
the power had gone off.
Kim walked away from the wreck
with nothing more than a gash on his arm.

It was his lucky day!

What goes up must come down

Up or down?

It was 1993 in France.
Dahran was 27 when he did
a parachute jump.
When he was 300 metres from the ground
it all went wrong.
A freak wind sucked him back up
into the clouds.
He went up faster than he'd come down.
He shot up over 10,000 metres.

The air was so thin he could hardly breathe.
It was 30 degrees below freezing.
The strong wind held him up there
for two hours!
He nearly passed out.
Then his parachute failed
and he fell back to earth.
He just managed to pull his spare parachute
before he passed out.

They found him only 30 miles
from where he'd first jumped.
They rushed him to hospital.
He didn't have any broken bones.
He had bad frost-bite and shock.
But he got over it.
He lived to tell everyone how
he'd once gone up in the world!

6
Nurse ... Help!

Hiccups

Did you hear about the man who had hiccups
for 68 years?
Charlie Osborne held the world record.
He started with a 'hic' in 1922,
and stopped with a 'cup' on 5th June 1990.
Some people have even died of hiccups –
including one pope.

Nasty things inside

A man went to the doctor with ear-ache.
The doctor looked inside
and saw lots of maggots.
They were feeding on the wax in his ear.
The doctor flushed them out.
They turned out to be from greenbottle flies.
The man got them from falling asleep
on seaweed at the beach.

Then there was the teenager in Turkey
who didn't feel too good.
She went to her doctor who took an X-ray.
It showed three water snakes living
in her stomach.
They were like string.
They were a foot long.

Three of these would definitely give you tummy ache!

An extra eye
Deng lived in China.
He was 23 when he went
to have his eyes checked.
The doctors couldn't believe their eyes.
Deng had three of them!
His third eye was on the left side of his head.
He couldn't see through it,
but it moved like his other eyes.

He was the third man in China
known to have three eyes.
That's a lot of eyes!

A story from the heart
A teenager in Hungary got into a bad fight.
He got a knife in his chest.
Doctors couldn't believe he was still alive.
The knife stuck out from his heart.

At least,
it was from where his heart *should* have been.
It turned out that his heart was on
the wrong side of his body.
Lucky for him!

7
What a Way to Go

Can it be true?
Did you hear about the thug
who made a letter-bomb?
He sent it by post to his enemy and waited.

And waited.

He watched the news.
He looked in the papers.
Nothing.

The problem was
he hadn't put enough stamps on the parcel.
It came back marked 'Return to Sender'.
When it landed on his mat
he was so pleased to get a parcel
he ripped it open and ...

got a BIG surprise!

A shot in the dark
Ken Barger always kept a loaded pistol
by his bed.
He kept it by the phone.
Just in case.
If a burglar called, he'd be ready.

But it wasn't a burglar who called.
It was his mum.
She phoned to say hello.
It turned out to be goodbye.

When the phone rang,
Ken woke up and went to grab it.
He picked up the gun instead,
and put it to his ear.
That was that.
He shot himself dead.
What a phone call!

Scary hairy
In 1988, Charles came to a nasty end.
It was all because of his fear of rats.
He hated them.
They scared him to death.

He lived with his wife in France.
One night his wife took off her brown wig.
She left it on a shelf in the bathroom.
Charles came in to clean his teeth.
He'd left his glasses in the bedroom.
His hand brushed against the wig.
He screamed.
He thought it was a huge rat
that had come up out of the toilet.
He was so scared that he fell on the floor …
and died of a heart attack.

A slip-up

In 1991, a crook went looking for cash in Spain.
He called at houses and tried to get let in.
He said he was a repair man.
A woman let him in.
Suddenly he grabbed her cash and ran.
She ran after him.
As he got to the door he tripped.
That was it.
He swallowed his false teeth
and choked to death.
Not a happy end.
Except she got her money back!

8
Almost the End

Some people are very lucky.
Just when it looks like their time is up,
they bounce back.

Dead woman moves
Mrs Jones fell face down in her bedroom.
She was in a deep coma.
Her family called the doctor.
He rushed round but it was too late.
He said she was dead.
They were all shocked.
It was awful news.
All they could do was call the undertaker
and the police.

As the funeral car pulled up
to their house in Yorkshire,
a policeman saw her leg twitch.
He took her pulse and gave her the kiss of life.
Before long she was breathing.

Mrs Jones was rushed to hospital,
and two days later she woke up.
Before long she was on her feet
and as right as rain.
If the policeman hadn't seen her leg move,
she would have been put in a body bag.
She would have gone to her funeral.

It was such an upset for the family
that in 2000 they got £40,000
for the awful mistake.

Back from the dead
Abdel fell into a coma in 1997.
He was in hospital in Egypt.
The doctors said he was dead.
They took him to a morgue
and put him in a coffin.
He woke up 12 hours later.
It was very dark so he pushed up.
The lid began to open.
He looked out.
There were bodies all around him.

He called out.
Some of the staff were laying out the bodies.
One of the workers looked up
and died of shock.
They had to lift Abdel out of his coffin
and put their dead friend inside.
Abdel walked off to have his tea!

So next time you read a story
and think it's too weird to be true
just remember:
The real world is more amazing
than you think.

Sources other than newspaper articles:

Fortean Times: *Strange Deaths, Close Shaves, Medical Mayhem*

Strange Tails: *All-too-true news from the animal kingdom* (Kohut/Sweet)

The Darwin Awards – Wendy Northcutt